TARGETING MUSIC

KEY STAGE 1 User's Guide

The *Targeting Music* books have been planned to link closely to the National Curriculum Programme of Study, and teachers have been promised stability until at least 2000 with regard to specified curriculum content. The charts in this booklet should therefore provide a secure framework against which to check your detailed planning - short, medium and long term.

There is a *Targeting Music* book for each year, starting with Reception, and a CD supplementing the first three books. The charts in this booklet show, chapter by chapter, song by song, which areas of the National Curriculum (England) are covered.

The charts make apparent the particular emphases in the Reception (pre Key Stage 1) book, and the way coverage then spreads across all strands as the series progresses. One can also see at a glance how the various lessons organize learning for the children as individuals, in pairs, in groups and as a whole classes.

The charts will serve as a checklist for **coverage**, to help fulfilment of legal requirements. They will also help you to maintain **balance** in your curriculum provision, and to plan for **progression**.

The authors do not claim that *Targeting Music* addresses every detail of the National Curriculum. However, as 'musical models' the series will be further supported by this booklet of charts - and further helped to guide this most fundamental stage of children's musical education.

The publishers wish to thank the copyright owner for permission to reproduce the Programme of Study for Key Stage 1 from MUSIC IN THE NATIONAL CURRICULUM. Crown copyright is reproduced with the permission of the Controller of HMSO.

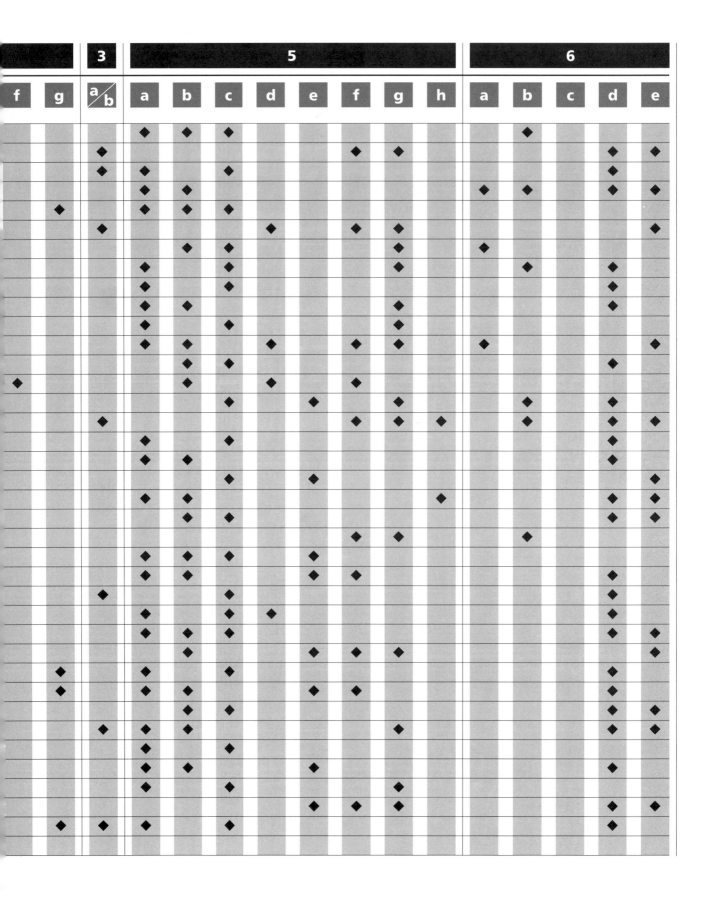

Targeting *Music*

Reception Year

Dorothy Taylor

Illustrated by John Minnion

SCHOTT
EDUCATIONAL
PUBLICATIONS

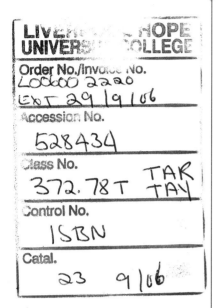
The author and publisher would like to thank Peter Nickol for his invaluable assistance in preparing this project for publication

British Library Cataloguing-in-Publication Data.
A catalogue record of this book is available from the British Library

ED 12445
ISBN 0 946535 26 4

Designed by Geoffrey Wadsley
Music set by Jack Thompson
Cover design by John Minnion

Contents

Introduction

Young children, on entering the reception class, bring very different musical experiences. Some have a repertoire of action songs, rhymes and games learned at home or nursery school; many do not. This heritage is essential as the root of music, dance and dramatic experience. Consequently, music teaching in the early years should focus on establishing musical experiences through and from this body of folklore, supplemented by new materials based on traditional structures. In the same way as the sensitive teacher bathes children in language, ideally he or she also bathes them in musical experience.

In this book, therefore, the principal aims are that children should be enabled to:
- experience music and musical activities;
- develop a repertoire of songs, action songs and singing games;
- cultivate a listening ear;
- develop sensitivity to music through the important skill of active listening.

However, this is a stage when children are being *gently* introduced to structured learning processes. Whatever particular focus runs through an activity, the establishing of pleasurable musical experience is our fundamental purpose.

Remember also that young children learn through imitating; you, the teacher, are an important role model.

The organization of the book

Although there is no need for strict adherence to the order of lessons, there is a sense of progression through the book, mainly in relation to the level of difficulty of the songs and the widening complexity of the related activities.

A song is, in almost all cases, the starting point for the lesson which follows. Development and progression are built into each lesson to enable it to be spread over two or three mini-sessions if this is appropriate. No hard and fast rule can be given about the length of time needed, as every musical encounter presents many possibilities and imaginative avenues for further development. In teacher-directed activities, it should be stressed that frequent short, concentrated sessions are better for young children than less frequent long periods.

Each lesson is spread over a double page. The vocal line is presented either unaccompanied or with piano accompaniment. There are chord symbols for guitar or autoharp which do not necessarily correspond to the harmonic progression provided in piano accompaniments.

A commentary running down the margin of the page provides an aide-memoire to musical processes and learning (left-hand margin), and general learning and cross-curricular links (right-hand margin).

Listening and responding

Listening is central to all musical activity; we listen, and we respond. Young children need constant opportunities to listen and actively respond to music – spontaneously and freely in their own way, and also through directed activities such as clapping, tapping or other co-ordinated actions.

They will find opportunities for both active and reflective response throughout this book. For example:
- various actions found in finger rhymes and action songs
- locomotor movements (walking, jogging, hopping, etc.)
- imitating a model (voice or instrument)
- listening and imagining (*My baby's crying*)
- listening and recognizing a rhythm pattern (*Move your fingers, move your thumbs*)
- listening for meaning (*In the morning*)
- listening for timing (*The body song*)
- listening and tracing in the air (*Up and down the staircase*)

Exploring, inventing and practising

These are natural human tendencies. Children need opportunities to play, explore, practise, rework, make and shape musical materials in structured and unstructured settings.

The lessons in this book present opportunities to:
- respond as individuals
- use imagination (*Sleep, baby sleep*)
- make decisions
- explore sounds and instrumental colour (*Roll the ball*)
- respond individually in free movement (*The elephant on a spider's web*)
- work imaginatively in pairs (*My name is Luke*)
- experiment with vocal sounds (*My animals*)
- investigate, explore, compare different sound sources (*Wind and sun*)
- extend classwork
- think of new words for a song (*Up and down the staircase*)
- build up a sound picture (*Train coming*)

Using the voice

Development varies greatly in young children, depending on prior experience and their growing ability to locate their voices physically and to match sounds. Never force this. It is quite usual for a group of young children to deliver a particular note across a broad pitch band.

At this age, the majority will sing within a restricted range of five to six notes. For this reason the repertoire here is predominantly in the range middle C up to A, though some of the songs go higher. Adaptations can be made, but often the aim should be to grasp the feeling and the rhythmic quality of the song rather than place undue emphasis on accurate pitch.

Young children learn much from teachers who sing with sensitivity to mood, accuracy of pitch, and with good diction, phrasing and control of breath. To improve children's singing dramatically, concentrate on good, even exaggerated diction. Children sing well when they stand rather than sit, legs firm and slightly apart, arms loosely at the side, so that their breath can be taken in and contained, supportively, in the lower part of the rib cage. Chins should never be raised, for this constricts rather than opens the throat.

There are many ways included here to use the voice, such as:
- chanting (Playing with sounds and rhythm – pages 10–11)
- experimenting with vocal sounds (*Wind and sun*)
- vocalising to 'loo' or 'la' (*My baby's crying*)
- singing, speaking, chanting (*Colours*)
- singing with a partner (*Sleep, baby sleep*)
- singing at different speeds or tempi (*Roll the ball*)
- singing expressively (*My animals*)
- matching pitch (*The swing*)
- singing an echo

Using the body

Physical response to music is natural in babies and young children. For older children, moving rhythmically to music helps to create a memory for musical patterns and features, to 'internalize' them.

Action and movement is pleasurable and expressive. It is a means of developing sensitivity to music in listening, performing and creating.

It may be used to develop a *rhythmic response* by promoting awareness of such things as steadiness of pulse, swinging or swaying 6/8 time, rhythm patterns, etc.

It is also helpful in fostering an *expressive response*, sensitizing children to the mood or character of a piece – is it light and airy? does it flow smoothly along?

Movement is also invaluable in encouraging a *creative response*, through imaginative individual and group movement improvisations and compositions.

Suggestions for movement range from actions of hands and feet in restricted space to paired activities and individual free movement. As children become confident as individuals with simple actions and movement patterns, they progress to the freer use of space, where walking, jogging and striding to music take time to mature. These locomotor movements require practice, balance and control.

Good use of movement promotes in the learner the skills of acute listening, concentration, co-ordination, energy control and memory training.

In this book movement suggestions include:
- rocking and swaying, individually or in pairs, from side to side (*My baby's crying*)
- tracing in the air upward and downward melodic movement (*Up and down the staircase*)
- clapping a partner's hands to a rhythm pattern (*Move your fingers, move your thumbs*)
- pulling actions (*Sail my ship*)
- walking steadily in time to the music (*Peter hammers with one hammer*)
- rolling a ball at different speeds (*Roll the ball*)

- patting and clapping rhythm patterns (*It's my birthday*)
- identifying a rhythm pattern by tapping it out (*Hush-a-bye my little babe*)
- expressive movement (*Worm*)
- joining hands in a circle, taking bouncy steps to left and right (*Join hands in a ring*)

Using instruments

Playing an instrument effectively is a most enjoyable experience. Technique and skills are required, however, to play even the simplest classroom instruments. Time is needed to 'play with', to explore, to practise and to refine.

At the infant stage, preparatory motor and co-ordinative skills should be developed before putting an instrument into a child's hands. Many physical actions are suggested in this book (such as walking, or tapping a steady beat) as part of this necessary preparation.

With singing at the core, classroom instruments are gradually introduced as appropriate. Care should be taken to show children how to look after (expensive) instruments and to be aware of their own safety (particularly if pairs of cymbals are used).

Apart from instruments made in the classroom (see *Adventures in Music for the Very Young* by Gillian Wakely, Schott's *Beaters* series), children need access to a range of good quality instruments.

Untuned:	hand drums, tambours, wood blocks, rhythm sticks or claves, triangles, cymbals, Indian bells or finger cymbals, tambourines, sleigh bells, maracas, guiros or scrapers, sandpaper blocks, cabasas
Tuned:	chime bars: C D E F F♯ G A B♭ B C (ideally more than one set, and with lower bars G A B) large bass bars (wooden): C, F and G soprano and alto xylophones and glockenspiels

The increasing range of interesting African, Latin American and Asian instruments enriches instrumental resources immeasurably, e.g. African thumb piano (*mbira*), gato drum, cow-bells, small Indian harmonium.

A good supply of beaters or mallets is necessary (rubber heads for chime bars, felt or wool for xylophones, wooden or fibreglass for glockenspiels). Again, children need to be shown how to look after beaters, ensuring that beater heads are secure and not allowed to work or remain loose.

Peter Sidaway's *Strike Five* in Schott's *Beaters* series contains excellent advice on all aspects of tuned percussion instruments and their use. Points to note are:
1) make sure that the longest (lowest) bars are on the left of the player;
2) if necessary, remove bars which are not needed (use both hands to grip them at each end);
3) bounce the beater on the middle of the bar so that it is allowed to vibrate.

Within this book instrumental work covers:
- playing rhythm patterns (*Hush-a-bye my little babe*)
- playing melodic patterns (*Sleep, baby sleep*)
- distinguishing between instruments (*Play the drum like this*)
- musical conversations (*My name is Luke*)
- playing an introduction (*The swing*)
- performing a steady beat (*Peter hammers with one hammer*)
- building sound pictures (*Train coming*)
- creating music in the music corner (*Wind and sun*)

Teaching a song

There are several ways of teaching a song. Teachers may find that they need to be flexible in their approach, and adapt these suggestions to their own teaching context.

The most direct way is by echoing back, when the teacher sings a line and the children imitate (see *I hear thunder*).

Another direct approach is to break the process into stages, first by chanting the rhythm or by getting the children to sing to 'loo' or 'la' (*It's my birthday*).

Very often, at this stage, the most natural or indirect way of teaching is to encourage children to join in – we say that the song is 'caught' rather than 'taught' (see *My baby's crying*).

Whichever way you choose, create a warm and confident atmosphere.

Accompanying songs

The majority are presented as a single melody line without accompaniment. Ideally the songs should stand alone, but chord symbols are provided should teachers wish to use a guitar or autoharp. There are piano accompaniments for some of the songs; some of these accompaniments incorporate the melody, but care must be taken not to drive the singing by playing the melody too loudly. An accompaniment exists to support and to enhance.

In addition, at the end of the book there is some piano music designed to accompany movement in a large space.

Organizing your lessons

Sessions will normally take place in the classroom – initially with the whole class, but also involving some group and individual work. This may be extended to other times of the day, with opportunities for continuing group and individual work within the classroom and in the music corner. Areas outside the classroom are often suitable for extending classwork, for example corridor space or the hall (particularly where locomotor movements are involved).

Single chime bars and hand-held percussion can be played standing or sitting, but glockenspiels and xylophones need to be played at a comfortable height on tables or on the floor with children kneeling in front of them. Whether in a group or as a class, much of the teaching will take place most effectively with children either sitting or standing in a three-quarter circle, maximizing eye contact.

Assessing and evaluating

You will wish to follow your own and your school's practice in recording achievement-levels. However, it is not suggested, at this foundation stage, that assessment should be a complex procedure. Bear in mind that children enter school with very different musical experiences, and some may have had little exposure to music of any sort.

Alongside the general evaluation of progress which should accompany lesson planning, a chart could be made to note individual participation, accomplishment or particular difficulty as they occur. In this way one builds a picture over a steady period. Such a chart, in producing a profile, will be useful for reporting to parents and recording the end-of-year picture for the receiving teacher.

Observation is the style of assessment suggested throughout. Areas to consider when noting the development of skills/abilities are:
- listening to music
- chanting, singing
- playing untuned percussion instruments
- playing tuned percussion instruments
- moving – in place, and freely
- discussing work
- exploring sound
- inventing music

9

Playing with sounds and rhythm

Musical learning

Feeling for rhythm and flow

Swinging rhythm

Rising melody

Steady beat

These well known and not so well known traditional rhymes and nursery songs are intended as introductory warm-up activities to the lesson models that follow. Through them, children will experience the rhythm of words and sounds, and the beginning of sensitivity in musical expression. There are also more general learning outcomes: acquiring vocabulary, and getting a 'grip' on words through articulating them clearly.

Round and round the garden

Round and round the garden,
Like a teddy bear.
One step, two steps,
Tickle you under there.

Row, row, row the boat

Row, row, row the boat,
Gently down the stream,
Merrily, merrily, merrily, merrily,
Life is but a dream.

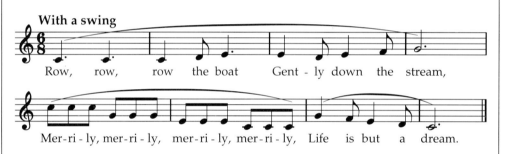

(For a piano accompaniment, see page 63.)

Hickory, dickory, dock

Hickory, dickory, dock
The mouse ran up the clock
      The clock struck one,
The mouse ran down,
Hickory, dickory, dock.
Tick, tock, tick, tock, tick, tock, tick, tock.

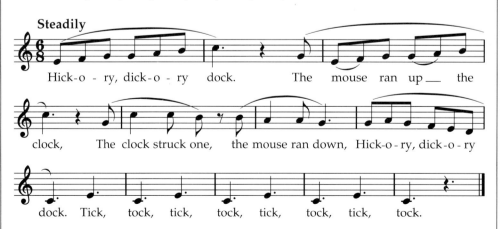

General learning

Speaking and listening

Acquiring vocabulary

Curling the **r**, *long* **o** *sound*

Dramatic action

Tongue exercise

10

Expressive
quality:
quiet and
mysterious

I know a house

I know a house,
A cold, old house
A cold, old house by the sea.
If I were a mouse in that cold, old house,
What a cold, cold, mouse I'd be.

Steady beat

Humpty Dumpty

Humpty Dumpty sat on a wall,
Humpty Dumpty had a great fall.
All the king's horses and all the king's men
Couldn't put poor Humpty together again

Clear
diction:
mouth
shape, use of
lips

Dramatic
play

Articulation:
distinction
between **p**
and **t**

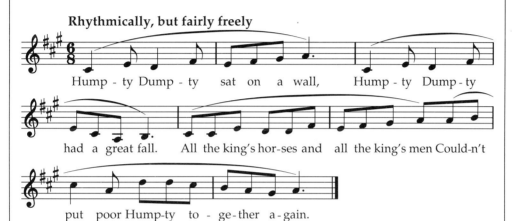

Rhythmically, but fairly freely

Hump - ty Dump - ty sat on a wall, Hump - ty Dump - ty

had a great fall. All the king's hor-ses and all the king's men Could-n't

put poor Hump-ty to - ge-ther a - gain.

Feeling for
rhythm
and flow

Doctor Foster went to Gloucester

Doctor Foster went to Gloucester,
In a shower of rain.
He stepped in a puddle
Right up to his middle,
And never went there again.

Holding the
vowel sound
(lines 2 and
5)

Expressive
effect of the
'Pop'

Pop goes the weasel

Half a pound of tuppenny rice,
Half a pound of treacle,
Mix it up and make it nice,
'Pop' goes the weasel.

Fun with
words

Jauntily

Half a pound of tup-pen-ny rice, Half a pound of trea - cle,

Mix it up and make it nice, 'Pop' goes the wea - sel!

(For a piano accompaniment, and a fuller version of the song, see page 64.)

1 My baby's crying

Musical learning

Feeling for swaying: 6/8 time

Feeling for melody

My ba - by's cry - ing, My ba - by's howl - ing. She went to bed an hour a - go And will not go to sleep.

1. My baby's crying,
   My baby's howling.
   She went to bed an hour ago
   And will not go to sleep.

2. We'll try and rock her,
   We'll try and rock her,
   She needs to know we love her so,
   And then she'll go to sleep...

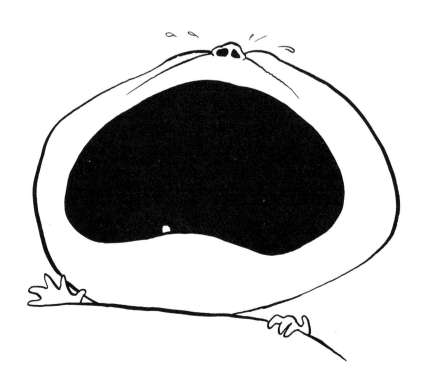

Listening and performing

Sing this lullaby quietly and smoothly. Your model will encourage the children to do the same. This is a little song to be 'caught' rather than 'taught'.

Ask the class to imagine that they are holding a baby sister or brother. Could they rock gently from side to side as they rock the baby?

After verse 2, encourage the children to continue to rock the baby while singing to the syllable 'loo'.

Finally, get everyone to stand still and watch carefully as you trace in the air the general upward and downward movement of the melody. Ask them to do the same.

Moving and performing

When the lullaby is well known, ask the class to make a circle with joined hands and rock from side to side, balancing first on one foot and then on the other.

Do this four times before starting to sing, yet maintaining the movement throughout.

Instrumental extension

Take a C chime bar and play a rocking ♩ ♪♩ ♪ rhythm to reinforce the physical movements. Do this a few times before inviting individual children to take a turn.

General learning

Caring for others

Physical co-ordination: rocking and balancing

Taking a turn

- ◆ Use of the syllable 'loo' in singing encourages good intonation.

- ◆ Tracing the general rise and fall of a melody helps to make melodic movement tangible and characterful.

Musical learning

Feeling for steady beat

Also for ♪♪♩ *rhythm pattern*

Controlling loud and soft

Alternating sound and silence

2 Move your fingers, move your thumbs

Move your fin-gers, move your thumbs. Put them on your tum, tum, tum.

Move your fin - gers, move your thumbs. Put them out of sight.

1. Move your fingers, move your thumbs.
   Put them on your tum, tum, tum.
   Move your fingers, move your thumbs,
   Put them out of sight. (*take behind the back*)

2. Where are my fingers? where are my thumbs?
   Where are my fingers? where are my thumbs?
   Where are my fingers? where are my thumbs?
   They're hidden out of sight.

3. Here are my fingers, here are my thumbs. (*bring them out again*)
   Here are my fingers, here are my thumbs.
   Here are my fingers, here are my thumbs,
   They're such a pretty sight.

Listening and performing

This is another action song to be 'caught' rather than 'taught'. Sing and perform the actions at a very modest speed.

Encourage the children to sing verse 2 very, very quietly, almost mouthing the words, in sharp contrast with verses 1 and 3.

When confident try these two alternatives which highlight the ♩♫ ♩ pattern:

1

2
In pairs, facing a partner, clap partner's hand each time the ♩♫ ♩ rhythm is reached – either *with* the sung phrase or *instead*, like this:

Listening and responding

Listen to part of the 'Russian Dance' from *Petrushka*, by Stravinsky. When they know the tune well enough, ask the children to clap along with the ♫ ♩ pattern, each time it comes.

◆ Many of these activities foster an appreciation of the need for *silence* as well as *sound* in music.

General learning

Co-operation

Concentration

Co-ordination

3 Sail my ship

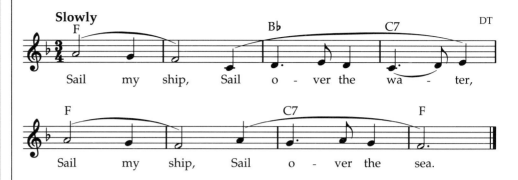

Sail my ship, Sail o - ver the wa - ter,

Sail my ship, Sail o - ver the sea.

Sail my ship,
Sail over the water,
Sail my ship,
Sail over the sea.

16

Listening and performing

This little song should be easily learned. Encourage the children to sing through the vowels:

> sai —l

and

> shi—p

Ask them to imagine that they are sailors pulling on the ropes to hoist the sails:

$\d.$ |$\d.$ |$\d.$ |$\d.$ |
Pull   pull   pull   pull

Invite a group to pull like this, four times, as an introduction to the song. They could chant the word 'pull' to reinforce each pulling action.

Instrumental extension

Later, transfer this pulling rhythm to chime bars, with one child to each bar:

$\d.$ |$\d.$ |$\d.$ |$\d.$ |
F   C   D   E

This can be an opportunity for children to respond to directions as they watch for the signal to play (first responding to you and later to individual children acting as conductors).

A frequent reminder of the rope-pulling action will help children to time their playing, as it promotes an internal picture (muscular memory) of the timing involved.

◆ Although some children will be eager to take a lead, others may need to watch until ready.

4 In the morning

Musical learning

Feeling for ♪ ♩.
rhythm pattern

Tempo: getting faster

♩ 𝄽 ♪ 𝄽 ♩ 𝄽

(sound and silence)

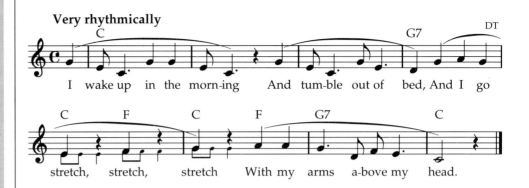

Very rhythmically

I wake up in the morn-ing And tum-ble out of bed, And I go

stretch, stretch, stretch With my arms a-bove my head.

1. I wake up in the morning
    And tumble out of bed,
    And I go stretch, stretch, stretch
    With my arms above my head.

2. I wake up in the morning
    And tumble out of bed,
    And I go munch, munch, munch,
    With my breakfast I am fed.

3. I wake up in the morning
    And tumble out of bed,
    And I go brush, brush, brush,
    Brush your teeth my mother said.

4. I wake up in the morning
    And tumble out of bed,
    And I go wait for me, wait for me, wait for me,
    As to school by Mum/Dad I'm led.

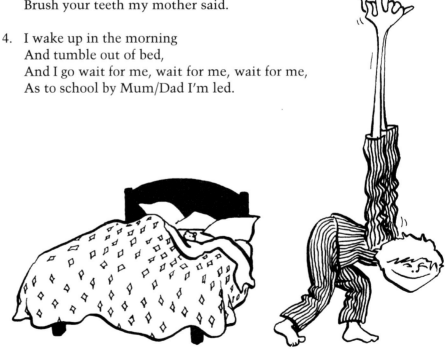

Listening and performing

Talk about all the things that we do when we wake up and get out of bed in the morning.

Now teach the first two lines of the song, and then alert the children to watch out for the different actions that the song suggests for each verse.

Act out the song verses with everyone standing in a circle. Practise the last verse, gradually getting faster over the last two lines. (But keep the acceleration under control, so that the performance remains rhythmical to the end.)

Listening and responding

Focus on the ♪ ♩. pattern, by clapping it every time it occurs. Then ask the children to listen as you go through a verse to see how many times the pattern appears.

Invite them to tap it out on their legs or on the floor.

Do the same with the ♩ 𝄾 ♩ 𝄾 ♩ 𝄾 pattern. (However, it may be
stretch stretch stretch
necessary to work for some time on the first rhythm pattern before attempting the second, perhaps leaving it to a subsequent session.)

Instrumental extension

Transfer one or both of the patterns to untuned percussion instruments such as claves or wood blocks.

General learning

English: speaking and listening

Mime

Counting

◆ Note how widely children differ in co-ordinating different actions.

5 Peter hammers with one hammer

At a steady speed

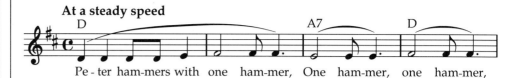

Pe - ter ham-mers with one ham-mer, One ham-mer, one ham-mer,

Pe - ter ham-mers with one ham-mer All day long.

1. Peter hammers with one hammer,
    (hammer on the floor with one fist)
    One hammer, one hammer,
    Peter hammers with one hammer
    All day long.

2. Peter hammers with two hammers,
    (hammer on the legs with two fists)
    Two hammers, two hammers,
    Peter hammers with two hammers
    All day long.

3. Peter hammers with three hammers,
    (both fists and one foot)
    Three hammers, three hammers,
    Peter hammers with three hammers
    All day long.

4. Peter hammers with four hammers,
    (both fists and both feet)
    Four hammers, four hammers,
    Peter hammers with four hammers,
    All day long.

5. Peter hammers with five hammers,
    (fists, feet, nodding head)
    Five hammers, five hammers,
    Peter hammers with five hammers
    All day long.

Listening and performing

Seat the children in a circle and encourage them to learn the song by following your example. There should be two strong actions or beats in each bar.

Through the accumulation of body percussion and energy there should also be a gradual increase in the volume of sound as the song progresses.

Listening and moving

Invite the children to walk around the room steadily in time with the music.

Encourage steady, deliberate strides (see the piano accompaniment below).

Instrumental extension

With a hand drum keep the steady beat. Demonstrate this before inviting individual children in turn to perform in this way – two beats to a bar.

Distribute four more drums and group the children in a semi-circle. (If you haven't enough drums, choose another untuned instrument which is relatively simple to handle.) Explain that this is the band, and that the drums are like the five hammers. Another child is invited to be the conductor of the band, and to bring in the players in turn as each verse is played and sung.

Listening and moving

Play the processional march from the last section of *Peter and the Wolf* by Prokofiev, and ask the class to stride slowly round the room in time to the music.

Optional piano accompaniment

◆ Some children will need more time and experience than others to develop the ability to perform a slow, steady, beat when walking and playing.

6 My animals

Musical learning

*Expressive quality;
loud and soft*

Tone colour

Moderate speed

My cat says 'purr'
Look at me
High in the sky
Up in the tree
Purr, purr,
You can't catch me!

1. My cat says 'purr'
   Look at me
   High in the sky
   Up in the tree
   Purr, purr,
   You can't catch me!

2. My dog says 'woof'
   Look at me
   Running round and round
   Flopping on the ground
   Woof, woof,
   You can't catch me!

22

Listening

Ask the children to think about the words of the song as you sing them. Focus on the qualities of both animals – the cat, smooth, sleek and graceful, and the exciting, chasing quality of the dog, as portrayed in this song.

Listening and performing

Teach the song two lines at a time. When secure, introduce the idea of singing the first verse more quietly than the second, to demonstrate the expressive qualities discussed earlier.

Inventing

Ask the children to think of different sounds that other animals make.

In turn, ask each child to demonstrate his or her chosen sound for others to guess.

Listening and responding

Taking a little drum or other untuned instrument, direct the children to make their chosen sound, in turn around the circle, whenever you play the steady beat on the drum.

Point out that whenever you stop or interrupt your playing, everyone suddenly must be quiet until you start again.

Then reverse the game. Whenever your instrument is played, everyone must be silent. When your instrument is silent, everyone squeaks, purrs, etc.

Provide children with opportunities to take your place, to be the teacher and to play the drum.

Listening extract

Listen to the love duet for two cats from *L'Enfant et les sortilèges* by Ravel.

General learning

Speaking and listening

Vocabulary: describing words

Controlled response to signals

◆ In the music corner, enable two children at a time to continue the activity of playing a drum and responding with different animal noises.

7 Roll the ball

Musical learning

Feeling for 6/8 rhythm

Varying the tempo (speed)

Varying the dynamics (loud/soft)

Exploring sounds: tuned percussion

With a swaying rhythm

Roll the ball, Roll the ball,
Roll - ing a - round and a - round.
Roll the ball to *Sa - rah,* Who
picks it up from the ground.

Roll the ball,
Roll the ball,
Rolling around and around,
Roll the ball to *Sarah,*
Who picks it up from the ground.

24

Moving

Make a circle with everyone kneeling.

Ask the children to imagine that they have a ball. (Specify a type and size that they are used to handling.)

Pretend that everyone is rolling the ball around just in front of them, keeping their hand lightly on the top.

Performing

Teach the song through repetition and action.

Introduce a real ball of a size familiar to the children. Alert the children in advance that you are going to roll it to one of them.

This time, when singing, roll it on the fourth line ('Roll the ball to.......') to the named child, who picks it up and brings it back, ready to start again.

Give other children a turn. When confident, ask individual children to take their turn in rolling the ball to others.

Listening and responding

When the song is well known, introduce different speeds – sing and do the actions quickly, very slowly, fairly quickly.

Use different dynamic levels – sing it quietly, with gentle actions, then sing it loudly, with vigorous actions.

Sound exploration

Encourage the children in the following:
- 'What happens when we roll a beater up and down a glockenspiel – all the way up, all the way down?'
- 'What happens when we do it gently?' – we get quiet sounds. What happens when we do it vigorously, slowly, quickly, etc?

General learning

Imagination/mime

Ball handling skills

Controlling fast and slow actions

Awaiting/taking turns

Vocabulary: relating to music

◆ Notice how both general and musical vocabulary are being fostered through these activities.

◆ While the interest will be in the 'fun' aspect of the song, a general feeling for the 6/8 swaying rhythm is steadily being established.

8 The swing

Musical learning

Swinging movements in 6/8 time

Fast/slow

Playing tuned percussion

Singing/echoing

Inventing 2-note patterns

Swinging, swinging,
Up in the air,
So high in the sky,
Push me and push me
And push me again.

Optional piano accompaniment

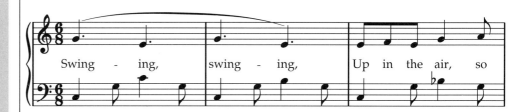

26

Ask the children to imagine that they are in or on a swing. How does it feel? Do they like being pushed?

Listening and moving

As you slowly sing the song, encourage the children to stand with one foot in front of the other, swinging their bodies gently back and forth.

On the second or third repetition ask them to pretend to push a swing – slowly, quickly, and in between.

Listening and performing

Once the song is being sung confidently, take two chime bars:

Play the first phrase as an introduction to the song:

$\downarrow.$ $\downarrow.$ $\downarrow.$ $\downarrow.$ |
G   E   G   E

Show how to bounce the beater off the bar, giving a clear resonating sound.

Ask individual children, in turn, to play the introduction; bring them round to sit behind the bars as they are laid out in front of them.

Listening and responding

Play G E, then sing the notes to 'loo'. Ask the children to match your vocal sound.

Do the same for E G and develop it further: G G E, E E G, etc. How many patterns can the class make in this way?

Encourage individual children to take a turn at being 'teacher'.

◆ The physical actions of swinging and pushing should add energy to the way in which the song is sung.

◆ Notice if there are problems with pitching sounds, and focus on this basic two-note calling pattern.

General learning

Physical co-ordination, balance

Mathematics: pattern-making and counting

Social development: awaiting/taking turns

9 Up and down the staircase

Fairly freely

Here we go... Up the stair-case, Up the stair-case, Up the stair-case,

Up the stair-case, Up the stair - case.__ At the top we

stop Take a breath be - fore we GO Down the stair-case,

Down the stair - case, Down the stair - case, Down the stair - case,

Down... At the bot-tom we STOP and FLOP!

Here we go...
Up the staircase,
Up the staircase,
Up the staircase,
Up the staircase,
Up the staircase.

At the top we stop
Take a breath before we GO

Down the staircase,
Down the staircase,
Down the staircase,
Down the staircase,
Down...

At the bottom we STOP and FLOP!

Draw a staircase on the flipchart or board.
Point to it as you sing this song to the class.

Listening and performing

Encourage the children to use their hands and arms to trace the climb and descent of the staircase as they sing in response to your signals.

Musical learning

Establishing a feeling for the rise and fall of pitch; singing up and down the scale; listening to observe pitch-changes

Musical pauses or resting places; singing with co-ordinated pauses (responding to signals)

Next, draw their attention to the physical sensation of their own voice as they feel it climb up inside them. Ask them if they can feel the vibrations.

Remind them of another song in which a little animal runs up and down (*Hickory, dickory, dock*).

Inventing

Help the children to think of new words and rhythms such as:

or:

Instrumental extension

Hold up a soprano glockenspiel so as to face the children like a ladder.

Show how the sound can climb up the ladder and down the ladder.

Invite the children to 'echo' the sound of the glockenspiel with their voices.

Help them to notice how the size of the bars alters as we climb higher and then come down again.

Talk about the 'vibrations' caused by the impact of the beater, and that the shorter or smaller the bar the higher the sound.

Encourage individual children to play going up and down the ladder. Get them to do it step by step and then play a game of putting in surprises where the rest of the class has to call out whether the sound has gone 'Up' or 'Down'.

Listening and responding

Ask the children to trace in the air the way in which the long sustained sounds move at the opening of Pachelbel's *Canon*.

◆ The concept of pitch being 'high' or 'low', 'rising' or 'falling', is an artificial one, so as many visual aids as possible should be used to foster and reinforce learning.

10 It's my birthday

Musical learning

Feeling for sprightly 2/4 time

pattern

1. It's my birthday, I am five,
   I am five,
   I am five.
   It's my birthday, I am five,
   Five years old today.

2. Light the candles on the cake,
   On the cake,
   On the cake.
   Light the candles on the cake,
   I'm five years old today.

3. Make a wish before you start,
   Before you start,
   Before you start.
   Make a wish before you start to
   Take a breath and blow them out! *blow*

This new birthday song might be sung by the reception class in an assembly.

Listening and responding

Pat the rhythm as you *chant* the words. Then sing the melody while gently patting out the rhythm.

Repeat until the song is known.

Listening and performing

When known, encourage the children to emphasize the line 'I am five' each time it occurs.

Mark the ♪♩ ♩ rhythm pattern by encouraging the children to pat it or clap it on each occasion. Ask if anyone knows how many times it is sung.

Instrumental extension

Transfer the ♪♩ ♩ rhythm pattern to an untuned percussion instrument such as claves (rhythm sticks), hand drum or guiro (scraper).

Provide opportunities for individual children to take a turn at playing this pattern.

Optional piano accompaniment

◆ Patting and clapping the rhythm pattern – i.e. using body sounds – ensures that the rhythm pattern is internalized before being transferred to an instrument.

11 I *hear thunder*

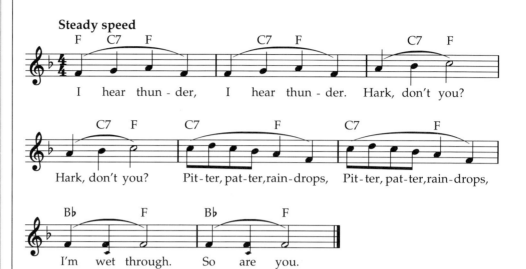

I hear thunder, (*teacher cups hand behind one ea*r)
I hear thunder. (*children do the same*)
Hark, don't you? (*teacher cups hand behind other ear*)
Hark, don't you? (*children do the same*)
Pitter, patter, raindrops, (*teacher shows action with hands and fingers*)
Pitter, patter, raindrops. (*children do the same*)
I'm wet through. (*teacher points to clothing*)
So are you. (*teacher and children point to each other's clothes*)

Listening and performing

Although known as a round, at this early stage the structure of this well known nursery song lends itself to being taught as an 'echo' song.

Ask the children to sing back, like an echo, each phrase after you have sung it. Do the actions; this reinforces the learning. Experiment with different dynamic levels, ranging from very quiet to reasonably loud.

When the song is well known, try reversing roles, with the children playing teacher or leader.

Instrumental extension

Draw attention to the 'pitter, patter, raindrops' pattern ♪♪♪♪ ♩ ♩ inviting the children to tap out the pattern with their two index fingers on the floor or on their legs.

Select, with their help, an appropriate untuned percussion instrument, such as claves or a shaker. Play the ♪♪♪♪ ♩ ♩ pattern all the way through as everyone sings the song. Invite individual children to take a turn.

Put this instrument in the music corner for individuals to explore in their own time.

Listening and moving

Play an extract from Debussy's *Jardin sous la pluie*, preparing the children to move to the music as if they were raindrops falling on the garden plants and flowers.

◆ By helping children to be discriminating when choosing appropriate instruments, sensitivity to the character of each individual piece of music is being encouraged.

General learning

Being leader, and follower

Imagination, imitation, mime; various locomotor movements

Selecting, discriminating

12 My name is Luke

1. My name is Luke
   What is yours?
   Will you play with me?
   I'll share my books
   And share my toys
   Then everyone will see
      We're happy!

2. My name is Rhiannon,
   I like you Luke,
   I will play with you.
   I'll share my books
   And share my toys
   Then everyone will see
      We're happy!

Listening and performing

Take three phrases at a time and teach the song by singing the words and tapping out the rhythm patterns.

When the children have learned it reasonably well, check to see if they can *think* the words while they tap out the rhythm of the song.

Choose two children to sing the song as a conversation, substituting their own names. While this is happening the rest of the class walk around in a circle in time with the music.

Instrumental extension

Humorously show how we could have a conversation without using any words at all, e.g. with body actions like claps, taps, clicks, stamps, etc.

Show how with facial gestures we can show various emotions like pleasure, sadness, anger.

Next, introduce pairs of instruments: pairs of hand drums, pairs of glockenspiels, etc.

Invite children to have different kinds of conversations – first using matching pairs of instruments and then contrasting pairs.

Optional piano accompaniment

◆ By thinking the words while tapping out the rhythm we encourage children to internalize musical patterns – hearing an internal aural image.

13 Sleep, baby sleep

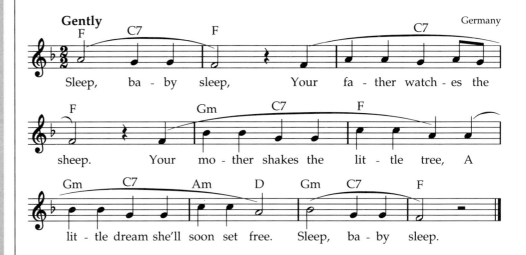

Sleep, baby sleep,
Your father watches the sheep.
Your mother shakes the little tree,
A little dream she'll soon set free.
Sleep, baby sleep.

Musical learning

Feeling for a lullaby; gentle 2/2 time

Recognition of melodic shapes

Song introductions

Playing tuned percussion

Like the Swedish lullaby which follows, the expressive quality of this German lullaby is mostly peaceful and gentle – although the middle section is more energetic, with greater movement, both melodic and rhythmic.

Listening and performing

Ask the children to imagine that they are rocking a cradle in which a baby is lying.

Teach the song, phrase by phrase, using the syllable 'loo'.

Ask if anyone notices anything about the central part (sing phrases 3 and 4).

Point out that the two phrases sound alike. Show the movement of the melody line by tracing it in the air.

Now introduce the words by first reciting and then singing them until the children have picked them up.

Listening and moving

Once the lullaby is well known, invite the children to take a partner. Standing face to face, get them to stretch their arms out in front and take hold of their partners' hands and sway from side to side while singing. (See the piano accompaniment opposite.)

Instrumental extension

Make a feature of the phrase 'Sleep, baby sleep'.

Put out the chime bars A G F and play  as an

introduction to the lullaby. Let the children decide how many times to play it. Ask if anyone would like to try to play it, while the rest of the class helps by singing the phrase slowly over and over again. This activity can also be explored in the music corner.

An important objective here is that the children should know what an introduction is, and know when to start playing and when to stop.

Optional piano accompaniment

> ◆ In the music corner, children will enjoy picking out the 'Sleep, baby sleep' tune, and making up other tunes from the three chime bars available to them.

14 Hush-a-bye my little babe

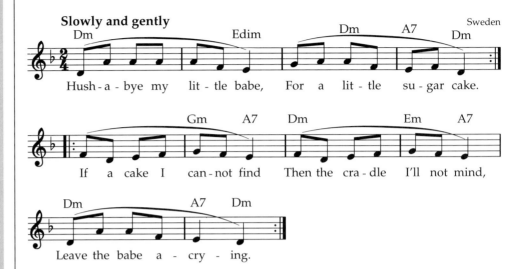

Hush-a-bye my little babe,
For a little sugar cake.
Hush-a-bye my little babe,
For a little sugar cake.

If a cake I cannot find
Then the cradle I'll not mind,
Leave the babe a-crying.

If a cake I cannot find
Then the cradle I'll not mind,
Leave the babe a-crying.

Listening and responding

Encourage the children to sway from side to side as you quietly sing this Swedish lullaby to them.

Ask them if they recognize what kind of song it is. Remind them of the other two lullabies in the book.

Listening and performing

Teach the song to 'loo' or 'la', and then to the words.

Pick out the ♩♫ ♩ rhythm as it appears at the end of every phrase, except the last where the lullaby comes to rest.

Tap it out, encouraging the children to imitate your action.

Sing the lullaby again and ask the children to tap out the rhythm pattern every time it arrives.

Ask if anyone can count how many times the rhythm pattern occurs.

Instrumental extension

Put out a selection of shaking instruments (bells, tambourines, etc.) and ask a group of children to choose an instrument each.

Invite the group to play the ♩♫ ♩ rhythm pattern while the rest of the children sing. Ask groups in turn to do the same thing until everyone has had this opportunity.

◆ The ♩♫ ♩ rhythm pattern or figure is the main characteristic of this lullaby, giving it a dainty, pointed, expressive quality.

◆ Timing in performance is encouraged through focusing on a particular pattern. Some children may anticipate too early, others too late. Bodily cues and signals give the necessary visual cues to help children to develop this skill.

◆ Help children to be selective in choosing appropriate shaking instruments. Encourage sensitive playing.

General learning

Counting

Sensitivity and control

Awaiting/taking turns

15 Our lollipop lady

Musical learning

*Feeling for swinging
3/4 time*

*Legato (smooth)
singing*

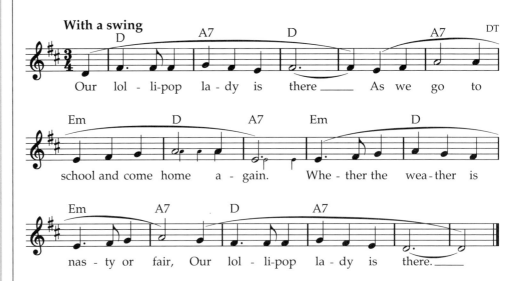

1. Our lollipop lady is there
   As we go to school and come home again.
   Whether the weather is nasty or fair,
   Our lollipop lady is there.

2. She says hello Kelly and Mark,
   She is always smiley, she's always the same,
   We want her to be there again and again,
   Our lollipop lady so fair.

40

Of course there are lollipop men as well; as in other songs, please adjust the words to suit your circumstances.

Listening and performing

Bring the children into a circle with joined hands.

Chant the first verse rhythmically for the children to imitate.

Encourage them to swing their arms (one swing to each bar) from side to side as they chant.

Next, teach the melodic line, demonstrating smoothness as the children repeat each line.

Moving

Draw one child into the centre of the circle to act out being the lollipop lady or man.

Encourage the rest of the class to join hands and walk jauntily around:

> first to the left (verse 1)
> then to the right (verse 2)

Instrumental extension

Choose children in turn to play a suspended cymbal in time with each step (one to each bar):

$$\text{𝅗𝅥. 𝅗𝅥. 𝅗𝅥. 𝅗𝅥.}$$

◆ Your model of smooth singing will help to develop this in the children.

◆ Expect to see differing rates of progress with respect to walking in time in a circle.

16 The body song

Musical learning

*Feeling for 4/4
walking time*

*Different ways of
using the voice:
singing, chanting,
speaking*

I have two strong feet, (*point to feet*)
I have two long legs, (*point to legs*)
They carry my body along, along, along,
I have two nice ears, (*point to ears*)
I have two bright eyes, (*point to eyes*)
And they help me to listen (*cup the ears*) and look and look and
    look. (*encircle the eyes*)

chanted: Feet and legs and ears and eyes
spoken: But what have I forgotten?

Two sturdy hands and arms besides. (*hold them out in front of the
    body*)

42

Start by asking the children to point to the different parts of the body: especially feet, legs, ears, eyes, hands and arms.

Listening and performing

Teach the song through action and repetition, performing it sufficiently slowly to be picked up as the actions are learned.

Listening and moving

When confident ask the children to follow you, as leader, around the room as you move in time with the steady beat, this time missing out the pointing actions.

Halt on 'But what have I forgotten', and remain in place until starting the song again on 'I have two strong feet'.

Movement extension

Build on the contrast between the static and dynamic parts of the song.

Using an instrument with a clear, distinct sound, practise moving and stopping.

Alternatively, page 62 contains sections of piano music designed to accompany walking, dancing and jogging. You may like to use these to accompany the moving-and-stopping activity.

- ◆ Notice how individual children begin to develop quicker responses to cues for actions.

- ◆ General alertness and co-ordination are encouraged as children respond to cues: stopping, starting, remembering to change from chanting to speaking, and then to singing.

General learning

Vocabulary: parts of the body

Actions: quick response

Sense of drama: contrasting movement and stillness

43

17 Play the drum like this

Musical learning

Playing untuned percussion; knowledge about the instruments – construction, tone colours

'Musical conversations'

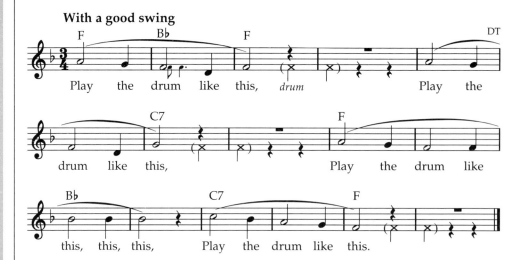

With a good swing

1. Play the drum like this,
   Play the drum like this,
   Play the drum like this, this, this,
   Play the drum like this.

2. Play the bells like this,
   Play the bells like this,
   Play the bells like this, this, this,
   Play the bells like this.

3. Play the chimes like this,
   Play the chimes like this,
   Play the chimes like this, this, this,
   Play the chimes like this.

4. Play the guiro like this,
   Play the guiro like this,
   Play the guiro like this, this, this,
   Play the guiro like this.

Listening and performing

Lay out in front of the children a drum, sleigh bells or bell tree, a chime bar, and a guiro (scraper).

Without directly teaching, sing the song and play each instrument in turn over the four verses as the song suggests.

Ask the children to pretend that they are playing the instruments just as you are. Repeat until reasonably well known.

While the children sing verse 1, assist an individual child to time his or her playing of the drum pattern.

Go through each verse, providing opportunities for children to take turns. Take time to show and talk about each instrument, and how it should be played to get the best possible sound.

Listen and discuss

Encourage the children to listen carefully and describe the different sounds that the instruments make: shaking, rattling, drumming, scraping and so on.

Extend this by talking about metal instruments and wooden instruments, and the differences between them.

Instrumental extension

Invite children to have musical 'conversations' between two similar instruments (for instance, two metallophones or two xylophones) and then between two contrasting instruments (for instance, metal and wooden, or plucked and scraped).

◆ Musical conversations present opportunities for children to explore instruments and their different tone colours in free rather than controlled situations.

◆ Children need time in the form of sheer 'play' to explore instruments: their characteristics and possibilities.

18 Worm

Musical learning

*Feeling for slow
steady beats*

*Feeling for melody,
pitch*

*Melodic contour:
descending scale*

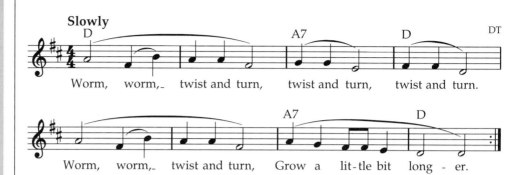

Worm, worm, twist and turn, twist and turn, twist and turn.

Worm, worm, twist and turn, Grow a lit-tle bit long - er.

1. Worm, worm, twist and turn,
   Twist and turn, twist and turn.
   Worm, worm, twist and turn,
   Grow a little bit longer.

2. Worm, worm, twist and turn
   Twist and turn, twist and turn.
   Worm, worm, twist and turn.
   Shrink a little bit shorter.

Listening and moving

Let the children 'catch' the first verse of this song through acting it out. As they pretend to be a worm twisting, turning from side to side, curling around, set the tempo by taking two slow steps to each bar.

When the song is well known, gather everyone into a circle and ask one child to stand in the centre and start the game. At 'grow a little big longer' he or she chooses another child, and together they start the song again until there is a long file of children. (If the class is too large for one line, work in two groups.)

Now teach the change of phrase in the second verse – 'shrink a little bit shorter' – as the first child leaves the line and drops back into the circle.

On another occasion, invite the class, as individuals, to take slow steps around the room, tapping the sides of their legs in time with their steps as they go.

Listening and responding

Now seated quietly, draw the children's attention to the sound of the last phrase, showing the descending movement of the last five notes by tracing it in the air.

Ask if this reminds them of any song they already know (*Up and down the staircase* – no. 9).

Encourage the children to imitate your action when reaching the last phrase.

Instrumental extension

Hold up a soprano glockenspiel with the notes D E F♯ G A.

Play the descending scale while singing to 'la' or 'loo'.

Invite individual children to come out and play it while the rest of the class sings the phrase.

General learning

Physical education: twisting, turning and curling

Co-ordinating two movements

Drama: role play, mime

◆ The activity of tapping legs combined with slow walking is good for co-ordinating two distinctly different activities, and needs to be practised.

Musical learning

*Tone quality:
exploring body
sounds*

*Exploring sounds
from everyday objects*

19 Put your hands together says Mrs Potato

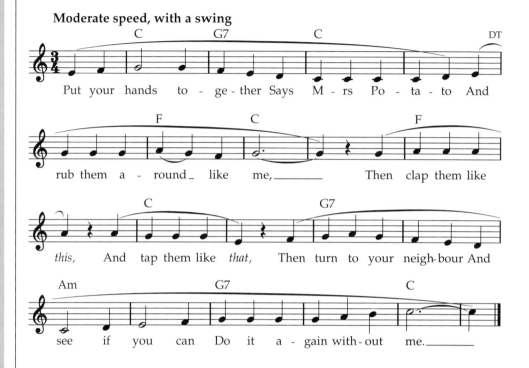

Put your hands together
Says Mrs Potato
And rub them around like me,
Then clap them like *this*,
And tap them like *that*,
Then turn to your neighbour
And see if you can
Do it again without me.

Listening and performing

Different sound qualities arise from these actions alone. Before teaching the song, practise putting hands together silently, rubbing, clapping and tapping. Then teach the song, line by line.

line 1: put the palms of your hands together quietly, without a sound
line 2: rub hands together in a circular motion
line 3: clap them together
line 4: tap one hand firmly with the index and middle finger of the other hand

As the song suggests, children turn to face each other and do the actions. This also encourages peer group learning.

On other occasions, invite some children to sing as individuals.

Adapting and inventing

Ask for ideas for new words. What could we do with our *feet*, for example?

Listening and recognizing

If you have a recording that prominently includes clapping, play this to the children. See if they can recognize the clapping action and respond by joining in. (Some possible recordings include *Clapping Music* by Steve Reich, *Eight days a week* by the Beatles or *Cecilia* by Simon and Garfunkel.)

Extension activity

In the music corner place materials which the children may explore by tapping together (dowel rods, bricks), rubbing together (sandpaper blocks, newspaper, foil), etc.

◆ Notice differing degrees of development with respect to co-ordination skills.

◆ Make a note of those children who readily wish to sing by themselves.

General learning

Vocabulary: describing different actions

Manipulative skills

Exploring: qualities of materials

20 Join hands in a ring

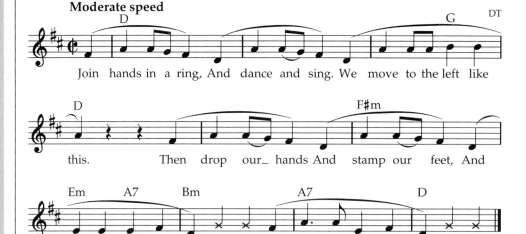

Moderate speed

Join hands in a ring, And dance and sing. We move to the left like

this. Then drop our_ hands And stamp our feet, And

clap our hands like this, *(clap, clap)* And clap our hands like this. *(clap, clap)*

1. Join hands in a ring,
   And dance and sing.
   We move to the left like this. (*side step*)
   Then drop our hands
   And stamp our feet,
   And clap our hands like this, (*loud claps*)
   And clap our hands like this. (*loud claps*)

2. Join hands in a ring,
   And dance and sing.
   We move to the right like this.
   Then drop our hands
   And stamp our feet,
   And clap our hands like this, (*quiet claps*)
   And clap our hands like this. (*quiet claps*)

3. Join hands in a ring,
   And dance and sing.
   We move to the centre like this.
   Then drop our hands
   And stamp our feet,
   And clap our hands like this, (*very loud claps*)
   And clap our hands like this. (*very loud claps*)

Listening and performing

Teach the song by doing it, for the actions trigger the words.

Listening and moving

Make a circle and take steady, yet bouncy steps first to the left (verse 1), then to the right (verse 2) and finally to the centre (verse 3).

At 'Then drop our hands' everyone stops moving, ready for the actions which follow.

Listening and focusing

After all this energetic movement, seat the children in a semicircle and focus

on the  pattern. Repeat it several times, emphasizing

the word 'this', to show how the claps follow the beat:

Then try some different actions:

> tapping on shoulders
> on knees
> on thighs
> on the floor

Play the 'Simon Says' game to establish learning in an enjoyable way.

Extension activity

Once this pattern has become internalized by most of the class, introduce an untuned percussion instrument, e.g. wood block or guiro, and play the pattern on it.

Sing the song through and let individual children take turns to play the rhythm pattern at the end of the last two lines.

General learning

Co-operation, co-ordination (for dance)

◆ Children of all ages, and particularly at this age, need time to explore the sounds of instruments and manipulate them. Put out a small selection of untuned instruments in the music corner for exploration.

21 Colours

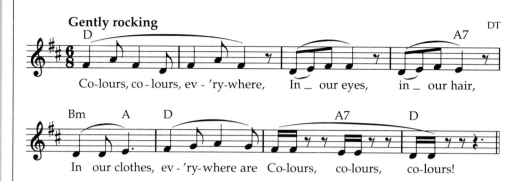

Spoken: Gemma, what is your favourite colour? *Gemma:* Red

Everyone chanting:

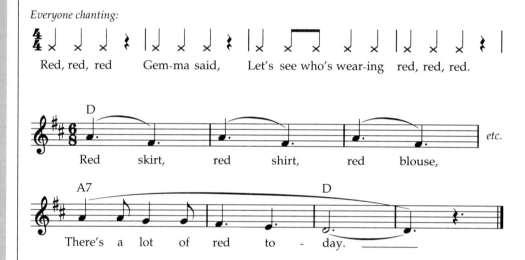

etc.

Colours, colours, everywhere,
In our eyes, in our hair,
In our clothes, everywhere are
Colours, colours, colours!

Spoken: Gemma, what is your favourite colour?
(*Gemma*): Red. (*or other colour*)

(*Everyone, chanting*): Red, red, red,
Gemma said,
Let's see who's wearing red, red, red.

(*Singing and pointing*)
Red skirt, red shirt, red blouse,
Red purse, red shoes, red pullover, *etc.*
There's a lot of red today.

52

With the children sitting in a circle or semicircle, set the context by finding out about their favourite colours, identifying them around the classroom and in the clothes that they wear.

Performing

As you sing the first part of the song encourage the children to move their bodies, on the spot, with a gentle, rocking motion.

Sing the first part again, and encourage the actions of pointing to eyes, hair, clothes, etc.

Then, address someone by name, and ask what is their favourite colour.

Teach the chant ('Red, red, red' – or whatever colour). Mark the rhythm by patting alternate knees or by tapping the floor on alternate sides, and ask the children to join in with this.

When judged to be appropriate, introduce the final part of the song ('Red skirt, red shirt' – or whatever).

An optional piano accompaniment for the first part of the song can be found on page 64.

Listening

Ask the children to listen to a piece of music about a girl with 'flaxen' hair: *La fille aux cheveux de lin* by Debussy (from *Préludes* for piano, Book 1).

◆ Notice how well the children are able to tap the rhythm of the chant.

◆ It takes time and practice to proficiently do two things at once, e.g. tapping and chanting simultaneously.

Vocabulary: colours, clothes

22 Train coming

Musical learning

Feeling for steady pulse

Then gradually getting faster, and gradually getting slower

Train coming,
Faster, faster, faster, faster,
Train coming,
Fast along the tracks.

Train coming,
Faster, faster, faster, faster,
Train coming,
Fast along the tracks.

Train coming,
Slower, slower, slower, slower,
Train coming,
Slowing to a stop. Whoosh...

Listening and performing

First teach this song as a rhythmic chant, moving your arms like pistons to show a steady beat. Next sing it, encouraging the children to join in, using their arms as pistons in the same way.

Moving in space

When well known, still performing at a steady speed, encourage the children to move freely in space as individuals. Practise stopping and starting.

Once this is achieved, encourage the notion of moving (and hence singing) faster and faster, then slower and slower.

Divide the class into two halves. While one half moves, the other half sings. Change over. You could use the piano accompaniment printed on page 63.

Instrumental extension

Introduce a swanee whistle for the final stopping signal.

Discuss steam engines – their noise, their huge wheels. Build up a sound picture of an engine using instruments.

Use a large suspended cymbal for

Use a two-tone wood block for

Listening and responding

Listen to Honegger's *Pacific 231* and invite the children to talk about what they hear.

◆ By asking half the class to move and half the class to sing, the teacher is able to assess how well they can carry out these activities.

23 The elephant on a spider's web

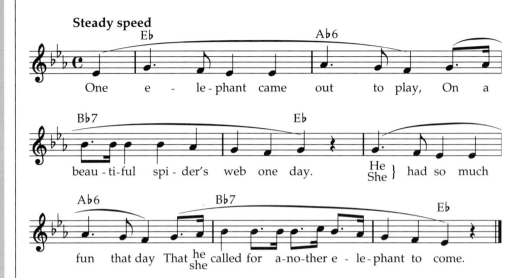

One e - le - phant came out to play, On a beau - ti-ful spi - der's web one day. He/She had so much fun that day That he/she called for a-no-ther e - le-phant to come.

1 One elephant came out to play
  On a beautiful spider's web one day.
  S/he had so much fun that day
  That s/he called for another elephant to come.

2 Two elephants...
  etc.

Listening and performing

This song is 'caught' rather than 'taught'. Before singing the song, talk about the notion of an elephant on a spider's web. Perhaps draw a picture. Discuss the size and weight of an elephant, and let the children freely imagine the graceful, precise movements of an elephant on a slender spider's web.

The song (originally French) has been adapted to avoid an unnatural stress on the word 'one'. In addition, by starting on an up-beat (anacrusis), necessary preparation time is given before beginning the walking action.

As teacher, play at being the first elephant, providing a role model for the class. Take slow, delicate tip-toeing steps, two per bar. At the end of the verse, take the hand of one child and lead off with the free arm extended in front to represent the elephant's trunk.

Enjoyment is the aim of this song, but the movements will help children gradually to develop a feeling for steady, regular pulse.

Later, faster movements, could be attempted, with four steps to each bar.

Free movement

Ask the children to listen to 'The Elephant' from Saint Saëns' *Carnival of the Animals* and show how the elephant moves.

Directed movement

Talk about the slow, steady way in which elephants move.

Play slow, regular strokes on a large, suspended cymbal and encourage the children to move like an elephant, taking long, slow steps as they listen to the steady cymbal sounds.

Encourage the children to move rhythmically, but avoid any anxiety about moving precisely in time with the cymbal beats. Your own movement example will gradually have its effect on the class and help them to move rhythmically.

◆ Notice which children listen well, and those who are able to control the way in which they move.

General learning

Physical education: controlled, delicate movement

Social skills: being a leader, being part of a group

Imagination: sense of fantasy, dramatic play

24 Splish, splash, splosh

Splish, splash, splosh,
Is the sound of the water,
Splish, splash, splosh,
This puddle's full of water,
Splish, splash, splosh,
As I trudge through the water,
What a good thing
I have my wellingtons on.

DT

Musical learning

*Exploring sounds:
water sounds, body
sounds, voice sounds,
word sounds*

*Focused listening:
environmental
sounds*

*Focused listening:
qualities of sounds*

Read the poem to your class and encourage children to play with the expressive quality of the words: 'splish, splash, splosh'.

Listening

Ask them if they can think of other water sounds, such as a dripping tap, water boiling, sounds of the sea, etc.

Let them listen to each other as they try to emulate the water sounds.

Next, consider sounds that people make. Demonstrate:
- with hands: clap
                rub
                tap
- with feet: stamp
                shuffle
                tap
- with voices: speak
                sing
                call

Suggest that we close our eyes for 60 seconds and LISTEN to all the sounds that are going on around us.

Then find out if everyone can remember these sounds in order (e.g. sounds of a door closing, distant traffic).

Extension activities

Collectively make a list for display of children's favourite sounds.

With a tape recorder show how the class can collect and record sets of sounds. For instance:
- a set of body sounds
- a set of classroom activity sounds
- a set of playground sounds.

Then discuss sound qualities in relation to:
- loudness/quietness
- getting louder/getting quieter
- single sounds, repeated sounds, constant sounds.

General learning

*Language:
vocabulary;
expressive qualities of
words*

Mathematics: sets

◆ The acute interest in *sounds* shown by children around the age of
two needs to be encouraged constantly throughout the early years.
This will help to counteract the daily aural bombardment of the
senses which leads to passive listening and problems of attention.

◆ Some children may need extra support in order to stimulate the
listening sense. This crucial activity is helped by asking them to
close their eyes when listening – especially focused listening (*for
something*).

25 *Wind and sun*

Musical learning

*Exploring sounds:
whispering, blowing,
etc.*

*Expressive qualities
of sounds: when
accompanying an
activity, or expressing
words*

The wind is *singing* through the trees
Like an excited *whisper*

With warm fingers *playing* on my face
The sun's rays *shine* through
As if they're *kissing* me

Soon I'll be five
I'm very much *alive*
Glowing in the sun
With the wind upon my face

DT

Listening and responding

Start the session by reading the poem.
Then ask questions such as:
- How does the wind sing through the trees?
- Can you whisper? (repeat the word, continuously)
- Are your fingers warm? Could we blow on them to make them warm?
- How would we make our fingers play on our faces?

Next, tell the children that you will play some sounds while they continue the last activity – fingers playing on faces.

Play gentle sounds at random. Try a glockenspiel (lingering, sustained), or a xylophone (short, dry), or an autoharp or guitar (plucked).

Sound exploration

Encourage the children to experiment with vocal and instrumental sounds.

Whispering Say the word 'whisper' in different ways:
softly, loudly, quickly, slowly,
all together, one after the other.

Shining sun Put out a selection of metal instruments: small
Indian bells, cymbals, triangles, glockenspiels.

In the music corner (reinforced with work cards and illustrations), suggest to the children that they make up their own music to accompany the poem; for example, music for 'shining sun', 'whispering wind', 'I'm alive'.

Listening and moving

Play the opening sequence of Ravel's 'Sunrise' from *Daphnis and Chloe* and encourage the class to respond by moving to it as if they were the sun.

- ◆ Notice the individual response of children to these tasks.

- ◆ Record which children engage readily in the listening tasks.

- ◆ Notice which children are keen to work in the music corner.

- ◆ Notice the way in which children generally respond to this poem and the qualities of sound and movement which it generates.

Music for walking

Music for dancing

Music for jogging

Row, row, row the boat

(see page 10)

Train coming

(see pages 54–5)

Pop goes the weasel

(see page 11)

Half a pound of tup-pen-ny rice, Half a pound of trea - cle, Mix it up and make it nice, 'Pop' goes the wea - sel! Up and down the Ci - ty Road, In and out the Ea - gle. That's the way the mon-ey goes. 'Pop' goes the wea - sel!

Colours

(see pages 52–3)

Co - lours, co - lours, ev - 'ry-where, In our eyes, in our hair. In our clothes, ev - 'ry-where are Co-lours, co-lours, co-lours!

USER'S GUIDE

a year-by-year series for teachers in primary schools

Dorothy Taylor

SCHOTT
EDUCATIONAL
PUBLICATIONS

KEY STAGE 1   Programme of Study

Pupils' understanding and enjoyment of music should be developed through activities which bring together requirements from PERFORMING and COMPOSING, and LISTENING and APPRAISING wherever possible.

1. Pupils should be given opportunities to:
a use sounds and respond to music individually, in pairs, in groups and as a class;
b make appropriate use of IT to record sounds.

2. When performing, composing, listening and appraising, pupils should be taught to listen with concentration, exploring, internalising, *eg hearing in their heads*, and recognising the musical elements of:

a PITCH - high / low

3. The repertoire chosen for performing and listening should extend pupil's musical experience and knowledge, and develop their appreciation of the richness of our diverse cultural heritage. It should include music in a variety of styles:

a from different times and cultures;

b by well known composers and performers, past and present.

b DURATION - long / short; pulse or beat; rhythm;
c DYNAMICS - loud / quiet / silence;
d TEMPO - fast / slow;
e TIMBRE - quality of sound
eg tinkling, rattling, smooth, ringing;
f TEXTURE - several sounds played or sung at the same time / one sound played on its own;
and the use of the above within
g STRUCTURE - different sections, *eg beginning middle, end;* repetition, *eg repeated patterns, melody, rhythm*

4.
Pupils should be given opportunities to:
a control sounds made by the voice and a range of tuned and untuned instruments

b perform with others, and develop awareness of audience, venue and occasion;

c compose in response to a variety of stimuli, and explore a range of resources, *eg voices, instruments sounds from the environment*

d communicate musical ideas to others;

e listen to, and develop understanding of, music from different times and places, applying knowledge to their own work;

f respond to, evaluate, live performances and recorded music, including their own and others' compositions and performances

PERFORMING and COMPOSING
5. Pupils should be taught to:
a sing songs from memory, developing control of breathing, dynamics, rhythm and pitch
b play simple pieces and accompaniments, and perform short musical patterns by ear and from symbols;

c sing unison songs and play pieces, developing awareness of other performers;
d rehearse and share their music making;

e improvise musical patterns,
eg invent and change patterns whilst playing and singing;
f explore, create, select and organise sounds in simple structures

g use sounds to create musical effects,
eg to suggest a machine or a walk through a forest;
h record their compositions using symbols, where appropriate.

LISTENING and APPRAISING
6. Pupils should be taught to:
a recognise how sounds can be made in different ways,
eg by blowing, plucking, shaking, vocalising;
b recognise how sounds are used in music to achieve particular effects,
eg to soothe, to excite;
c recognise that music comes from different times and places;

d respond to musical elements, and the changing character and mood of a piece of music by means of dance or other suitable forms of expression;
e describe in simple terms the sounds they have made, listened to, performed, composed or heard, including everyday sounds.

User's Guide

Reception Year and Years 1 & 2

a year-by-year series for teachers in primary schools

Dorothy Taylor and Jo Brockis

780

SCHOTT
EDUCATIONAL
PUBLICATIONS

Programme of study: MUSIC

Key stage 1

Knowledge, skills and understanding

Teaching should ensure that **listening, and applying knowledge and understanding**, are developed through the interrelated skills of **performing, composing** and **appraising**.

Controlling sounds through singing and playing – performing skills

1 Pupils should be taught to:
   a use their voices expressively by singing songs and speaking chants and rhymes
   b play tuned and untuned instruments
   c rehearse and perform with others (for example, starting and finishing together, keeping to a steady pulse).

Creating and developing musical ideas – composing skills

2 Pupils should be taught how to:
   a create musical patterns
   b explore, choose and organise sounds and musical ideas.

Responding and reviewing – appraising skills

3 Pupils should be taught how to:
   a explore and express their ideas and feelings about music using movement, dance and expressive and musical language
   b make improvements to their own work.

Listening, and applying knowledge and understanding

4 Pupils should be taught:
   a to listen with concentration and to internalise and recall sounds with increasing aural memory
   b how the combined musical elements of pitch, duration, dynamics, tempo, timbre, texture and silence can be organised and used expressively within simple structures (for example, beginning, middle, end)
   c how sounds can be made in different ways (for example, vocalising, clapping, by musical instruments, in the environment) and described using given and invented signs and symbols
   d how music is used for particular purposes (for example, for dance, as a lullaby).

Breadth of study

5 During the key stage, pupils should be taught the Knowledge, skills and understanding through:
   a a range of musical activities that integrate performing, composing and appraising
   b responding to a range of musical and non-musical starting points
   c working on their own, in groups of different sizes and as a class
   d a range of live and recorded music from different times and cultures.

During key stage 1 pupils listen carefully and respond physically to a wide range of music. They play musical instruments and sing a variety of songs from memory, adding accompaniments and creating short compositions, with increasing confidence, imagination and control. They explore and enjoy how sounds and silence can create different moods and effects.

1a → links to other subjects
This requirement builds on En1/1a, 8b.

2b → ICT opportunity
Pupils could use software designed to enable exploration of sounds.

3a → links to other subjects
This requirement builds on En1/4a and PE/6a, 6c

3b → ICT opportunity
Pupils could use recording equipment to recall sounds and identify and make improvements.

Note for 4
Listening is integral to the development of all aspects of pupils' knowledge and understanding of music.

4a → links to other subjects
This requirement builds on En1/2a, 2f

4b, 4c → links to other subjects
These requirements build on Sc4/3c, 3d.

Note for 4b
• pitch – higher/lower
• duration – longer/shorter steady pulse, beat, rhythm
• dynamics – louder/quieter/silence
• tempo – faster/slower
• timbre – different types of sound
• texture – different ways sounds are combined
• structure – different ways sounds are organised.

5b → links to other subjects
This requirement builds on En2/3b, 3d-3f and PE/6a-6c.

TARGETING MUSIC

User's Guide

KEY STAGE 1

The *Targeting Music* book series has been planned to link closely with the National Curriculum Programmes of Study. This User's Guide replaces the original guidance to match the revised legal requirements in England for the National Curriculum for music, implemented in 2000.

There is a *Targeting Music* book for each year starting with Reception and ending with Year 6. A compact disc is available containing all the music and listening extracts in the three books for Key Stage 1. At Key Stage 2 a disc covering the listening extracts for years 3 and 4, and a comparable one for years 5 and 6, is attached to the back cover.

The charts in this pamphlet show, chapter by chapter, lesson by lesson, which areas of the National Curriculum (England) are **covered.** They will serve as a checklist to help you fulfil broad statutory requirements. They will also support you in maintaining **balance** of curriculum provision and in planning for **progression.**

In the first two books (reception and year 1) the charts make apparent particular emphases and the way coverage then spreads across all strands as the series progresses. From year 2 onwards a modular construction enables one to see, at a glance, the particular modular focus and its integration with other programmes of study.

The authors do not intend the *Targeting Music* series to be a substitute for a scheme of work. However, as a progressive, year by year set of 'musical models' the series should provide ample support for implementing teachers' schemes of work and, as wide ranging, year by year materials be further supported by this booklet of charts.

The publishers wish to thank the copyright owner for permission to reproduce the programme of Study for Key Stage 1 from MUSIC IN THE NATIONAL CURRICULUM. © The Queen's Printer and Controller of HMSO. Reproduced under the terms of HMSO Guidance Note 8.

YEAR 1

Programmes of study
TARGETING MUSIC

	1			2		3		4			
	A	B	C	A	B	A	B	A	B	C	D
1. Round and round the garden	♦		♦						♦		
2. Round and round (dev.)	♦		♦		♦	♦			♦		
3. Hey diddle diddle	♦		♦		♦	♦			♦		
4. Hey diddle (dev.)	♦		♦			♦			♦		
5. Little wind	♦			♦	♦				♦		
6. Little wind (dev.)	♦	♦	♦	♦	♦			♦			
7. Father and Mother and Uncle John	♦	♦			♦				♦		
8. Father and Mother (dev.)	♦		♦						♦		
9. Two little birds	♦						♦		♦		
10. Two little birds (dev.)	♦					♦		♦	♦		
11. Incy Wincy Spider	♦						♦	♦			
12. Incy Wincy Spider (dev.)	♦	♦	♦		♦	♦					
13. Christmas bells	♦				♦	♦		♦			
14. Christmas bells (dev.)		♦	♦			♦		♦	♦		
15. Jack Frost	♦	♦				♦					
16. Jack Frost (dev.)		♦			♦	♦		♦		♦	
17. Five currant buns	♦		♦			♦		♦			
18. Five currant buns (dev.)	♦	♦				♦			♦		
19. I'm a little teapot	♦					♦			♦	♦	
20. I'm a little teapot (dev.)								♦		♦	
21. Hands are meant to clap	♦	♦	♦								
22. Hands are meant to clap (dev.)		♦		♦	♦				♦		
23. Mandy stands so big and tall	♦	♦	♦						♦		
24. Mandy stands so big and tall (dev.)	♦	♦		♦				♦	♦		
25. Just like me	♦		♦			♦			♦		
26. Just like me (dev.)	♦					♦		♦			
27. The bear went over the mountain	♦	♦							♦		
28. The bear (dev.)	♦	♦	♦	♦	♦	♦					
29. Who made the pie?	♦		♦						♦		
30. Who made the pie? (dev.)	♦	♦				♦		♦			
31. Stars	♦	♦						♦	♦		♦
32. Stars (dev.)	♦	♦				♦		♦			
33. Cats and dogs	♦					♦					
34. Cats and dogs (dev.)				♦				♦	♦		
35. Little frog	♦							♦			
36. Little frog (dev.)		♦		♦				♦	♦		
37. The band in the park	♦	♦				♦		♦			
38. The band (dev.)	♦	♦			♦	♦					

RECEPTION YEAR

The National Curriculum KEY STAGE 1 Programme of Study
The continuous strand represented by programme of study 5:
Breadth of study is not included here as the opportunity and
entitlement which it represents are intrinsic to the contents of
the books

Programmes of study
TARGETING MUSIC

	1			2		3		4			
	A	B	C	A	B	A	B	A	B	C	D
Playing with sounds and rhythm	◆		◆						◆		
1. My baby's crying	◆	◆	◆			◆			◆		
2. Move your fingers, move your thumbs	◆		◆			◆		◆	◆		
3. Sail my ship	◆	◆	◆						◆		
4. In the morning	◆	◆	◆						◆	◆	
5. Peter hammers with one hammer	◆	◆	◆						◆		
6. My animals	◆		◆	◆				◆	◆		
7. Roll the ball	◆		◆		◆				◆		
8. The swing	◆	◆				◆			◆		
9. Up and down the staircase				◆					◆		
10. It's my birthday	◆	◆				◆					
11. I hear thunder	◆	◆				◆		◆	◆		
12. My name is Luke	◆				◆	◆			◆		
13. Sleep, baby, sleep		◆				◆			◆		◆
14. Hush-a-bye my little babe	◆	◆	◆						◆		◆
15. Our lollipop lady	◆	◆	◆						◆		
16. The body song									◆		
17. Play the drum like this	◆	◆			◆					◆	
18. Worm	◆	◆	◆					◆	◆		
19. Put your hands together	◆	◆	◆					◆	◆		
20. Join hands in a ring	◆								◆		
21. Colours	◆			◆					◆		
22. Train coming	◆		◆				◆	◆	◆		
23. The elephant on a spider's web	◆					◆			◆		
24. Splish, splash, splosh					◆			◆			
25. Wind and sun					◆	◆					

YEAR 2

The National Curriculum KEY STAGE 1 Programme of Study
The continuous strand represented by programme of study 5: Breadth of study is not included here as the opportunity and entitlement which it represents are intrinsic to the contents of the books

Programmes of study
TARGETING MUSIC

	1 A	1 B	1 C	2 A	2 B	3 A	3 B	4 A	4 B	4 C	4 D
MODULE 1: DYNAMICS											
1. Lovely things	◆	◆	◆			◆	◆	◆			
2. Lovely things (dev.)	◆	◆	◆	◆	◆			◆	◆	◆	
3. The animal kingdom	◆			◆	◆	◆		◆			
4. I can sing quietly	◆					◆	◆	◆	◆		
5. In the distance		◆		◆		◆		◆	◆		
6. The wheel never stops	◆	◆			◆	◆		◆			
MODULE 2: PITCH											
1. The up and down song	◆	◆		◆				◆			
2. Little red bird: a Manx lullaby	◆		◆			◆		◆			◆
3. Little red bird (dev.)	◆	◆	◆		◆	◆	◆	◆			◆
4. Happy Divali	◆	◆			◆		◆	◆	◆		◆
5. Chanukkah candles					◆			◆	◆	◆	◆
6. Gentle donkey	◆	◆		◆			◆				
MODULE 3: RHYTHM											
1. Oliver Twist	◆			◆	◆	◆		◆			
2. Oliver Twist (dev.)	◆		◆	◆		◆		◆		◆	
3. I'm a magician	◆	◆		◆				◆			
4. Are you sleeping?	◆	◆				◆		◆			
5. Sur le pont d'Avignon	◆					◆		◆			
6. Poems and stories as stimuli for composing		◆		◆	◆				◆		
MODULE 4: TIMBRE OR TONE QUALITY											
1. Lots of different sounds	◆				◆			◆		◆	
2. Lots of different sounds (dev.)					◆		◆				
3. Ting, tap, crash	◆	◆									
4. Sound discoveries		◆			◆	◆		◆			
5. Sounds from across the world	◆	◆				◆					◆
6. Moving mode	◆	◆			◆	◆		◆			
MODULE 5: TEXTURE											
1. Sounds around	◆				◆			◆			
2. Sound layers	◆	◆				◆				◆	
3. Togetherness	◆	◆						◆			
4. Building sounds		◆			◆						
5. Turn the glasses over	◆	◆							◆		
6. Rainbow colours	◆				◆						
MODULE 6: STRUCTURE											
1. Who's that yonder	◆	◆			◆			◆	◆		
2. Hush little baby	◆	◆	◆		◆			◆			
3. John Brown's body	◆				◆			◆	◆	◆	◆
4. A ram sam sam	◆	◆	◆					◆			
5. More rounds	◆	◆			◆						
6. Wedding day at Troldhaugen				◆	◆			◆	◆	◆	◆

TARGETING MUSIC

S28434
Barcode on Page 6

A year-by-year series for teachers in primary schools

A major new series of books initiated by Dorothy Taylor, addressing the needs of the music curriculum in primary education. Assembled for use by teachers without specialist training but wishing to use their own abilities – however modest, as singers or players – to deliver a musically rich diet to classes in their charge.

Key Stage 1 User's Guide

Inside this booklet you will find charts to help you plot usage of the Targeting Music books and CD against coverage of the National Curriculum (England)

Reception year (age 4-5) ED 12445
Dorothy Taylor

This first book in the series has plentiful guidance for the teacher. It lays a foundation of musical experience through integrated activities and a repertoire of songs and singing games. It aims throughout to encourage a natural and enjoyable feeling for rhythm and music and to cultivate a sensitive, listening ear.

Year 1 (age 5-6) ED 12449
Dorothy Taylor

Building on the book for Reception year these 38 model lessons (devised in pairs) approach music through the fundamental musical experiences: exploring and creating; listening and performing. The encouragement of active listening is central.

Year 2 (age 6-7) ED 12456
Dorothy Taylor and Jo Brockis

In the third book of the series a six modular structure is adopted to develop more sustained and challenging learning experiences in Year 2. Attuned to the National Curriculum, content is organised through a focus on: dynamics; pitch; rhythm; timbre or tone quality; texture; structure

A CD (**ED 12483**) is available to supplement the first three *Targeting Music* books (covering the infant years). It contains all of the original songs, and also short extracts covering most of the listening suggestions in the text.

Dorothy Taylor is one of our foremost educators. She has extensive teaching experience in primary schools, and compiled the *Learning with Traditional Rhymes* series for Ladybird Books, as well as being the author, co-author and editor of books and articles on music education. For eleven years she was a lecturer in music education at the University of London Institute of Education, before moving into local education authority advisory and inspection work. Recently retired, she continues to work as a consultant and author.

Jo Brockis is Adviser for Music with the Essex Development and Advisory Service. She has taught in both primary and secondary schools and has considerable experience in music advisory work for primary schools.

SCHOTT

48 Great Marlborough Street, London W1F 7BB
Tel: 020 7437 1246 Fax: 020 7437 0263

Marketing/Sales Department: Brunswick Road, Ashford, Kent TN23 1DX
Tel: (01233) 628987 Fax: (01233) 610232

TARGETING MUSIC

	1 a (1)	1 a (2)	1 a (G)	1 a (C)	1 b	2 a	2 b	2 c	2 d	2 e	2 f	2 g	3 a/b	5 a	5 b	5 c	5 d	5 e	5 f	5 g	5 h	6 a	6 b	6 c	6 d	6 e
MODULE 1 - Dynamics																										
1. Lovely things	◆			◆				◆					◆	◆	◆	◆	◆									◆
2. Lovely things (development)	◆		◆					◆						◆	◆			◆	◆		◆					
3. The animal kingdom			◆	◆			◆	◆		◆						◆				◆						◆
4. I can sing quietly			◆	◆				◆	◆	◆			◆							◆						◆
5. In the distance	◆							◆								◆		◆				◆				◆
6. The wheel never stops	◆	◆	◆	◆				◆			◆		◆			◆			◆	◆					◆	
MODULE 2 - Pitch				◆																						
1. The up and down song	◆					◆												◆	◆		◆					
2. Little red bird: a Manx lullaby						◆	◆			◆			◆			◆	◆							◆	◆	
3. Little red bird (development)	◆		◆	◆		◆						◆	◆			◆										
4. Happy Divali	◆		◆	◆		◆					◆		◆					◆								
5. Chanukkah candles	◆		◆	◆		◆					◆		◆					◆		◆			◆			
6. Gentle donkey	◆		◆	◆		◆																				
MODULE 3 - Rhythm				◆																						
1. Oliver Twist	◆		◆				◆		◆				◆			◆		◆							◆	◆
2. Oliver Twist (development)			◆	◆			◆						◆	◆		◆										◆
3. I'm a magician	◆						◆				◆	◆				◆	◆									◆
4. Are you sleeping	◆		◆	◆			◆						◆													◆
5. Sur le pont d'Avignon							◆				◆		◆			◆										◆
6. Poems and stories as stimuli for composing			◆	◆			◆										◆	◆		◆						◆
MODULE 4 - Timbre or tone quality				◆																						
1. Lots of different sounds	◆									◆					◆	◆						◆				◆
2. Lots of different sounds (development)			◆	◆						◆						◆		◆		◆						◆
3. Ting, tap, crash			◆	◆						◆						◆				◆		◆				◆
4. Sound discoveries			◆	◆						◆						◆		◆				◆		◆		◆
5. Sounds from across the world			◆	◆						◆			◆			◆								◆		◆
6. Moving mode			◆	◆						◆		◆	◆			◆		◆							◆	◆
MODULE 5 - Texture				◆																						
1 Sounds around	◆	◆	◆				◆			◆	◆					◆										◆
2. Sound layers			◆	◆			◆			◆						◆	◆				◆					
3. Togetherness	◆	◆								◆	◆	◆					◆									
4. Building sounds											◆					◆		◆								
5. Turn the glasses over	◆	◆					◆				◆	◆	◆												◆	
6. Rainbow colours	◆		◆								◆			◆				◆						◆		
MODULE 6 - Structure				◆													◆									
1. Who's that yonder	◆	◆	◆			◆							◆	◆		◆		◆	◆							
2. Hush little baby			◆	◆									◆	◆		◆								◆		◆
3. John Brown's body			◆	◆									◆						◆	◆	◆			◆	◆	◆
4. A ram sam sam	◆	◆	◆	◆							◆		◆	◆		◆										
5. More rounds			◆	◆							◆	◆		◆		◆				◆				◆		◆
6. Wedding day at Troldhaugen																	◆									

The National Curriculum
KEY STAGE 1 Programme of Study

The continuous strands represented by Programme of Study No. 4 (applying to all key stages) are not included here, as the opportunity and entitlement which they represent receive a more detailed and age-specific statement in Nos. 5 and 6

		3		5									6				
f	g	a/b	a	b	c	d	e	f	g	h	a	b	c	d	e
					◆				◆			◆			
	◆		◆	◆							◆			◆	
					◆									◆	
				◆					◆						
				◆										◆	
◆														◆	
	◆				◆		◆					◆			
	◆			◆	◆			◆							
◆				◆			◆		◆			◆			
	◆				◆	◆						◆			◆
			◆	◆	◆	◆									
	◆			◆	◆		◆					◆			
◆			◆		◆		◆					◆			
				◆	◆			◆				◆			
				◆	◆				◆			◆			
			◆		◆							◆			
			◆		◆							◆			
			◆	◆	◆			◆		◆				◆	
	◆			◆	◆							◆		◆	
◆		◆		◆	◆							◆		◆	
◆		◆		◆	◆				◆			◆			
	◆			◆	◆		◆					◆			

TARGETING MUSIC

	1				2				
	a			**b**	**a**	**b**	**c**	**d**	**e**
	1 2 G C								
1. Round and round the garden	◆		◆		◆	◆			◆
2. Round and round the garden (development)	◆		◆		◆	◆			◆
3. Hey diddle diddle	◆		◆		◆	◆			◆
4. Hey diddle diddle (development)	◆		◆		◆	◆			◆
5. Little wind	◆		◆		◆	◆			◆
6. Little wind (development)	◆		◆		◆	◆			◆
7. Father and Mother and Uncle John	◆		◆		◆	◆			◆
8. Father and Mother and Uncle John (dev.)			◆		◆	◆		◆	◆
9. Two Little birds			◆		◆	◆			◆
10. Two Little birds (development)	◆ ◆		◆		◆	◆			
11. Incy Wincy Spider	◆		◆		◆	◆			
12. Incy Wincy Spider (development)	◆ ◆		◆		◆	◆			
13. Christmas bells	◆		◆		◆		◆		
14. Christmas bells (development)	◆	◆	◆		◆				
15. Jack Frost	◆		◆		◆				◆
16. Jack Frost (development)			◆						
17. Five currant buns	◆		◆		◆	◆			◆
18. Five currant buns (development)	◆		◆		◆	◆			◆
19. I'm a little teapot			◆		◆	◆		◆	
20. I'm a little teapot (development)	◆		◆		◆	◆			
21. Hands are meant to clap	◆ ◆		◆		◆			◆	
22. Hands are meant to clap (development)		◆	◆		◆				◆
23. Mandy stands so big and tall			◆		◆				
24. Mandy stands so big and tall (development)	◆ ◆ ◆ ◆		◆		◆				
25. Just like me			◆		◆	◆		◆	
26. Just like me (development)	◆		◆		◆	◆		◆	
27. The bear who went over the mountain	◆		◆		◆	◆		◆	
28. The bear who went over the mountain (dev.)	◆ ◆		◆		◆	◆			◆
29. Who made the pie?	◆	◆	◆		◆	◆			
30. Who made the pie? (development)	◆ ◆		◆		◆	◆			
31. Stars	◆		◆		◆		◆		◆
32. Stars (development)	◆		◆		◆		◆	◆	
33. Cats and dogs			◆		◆			◆	
34. Cats and dogs (development)	◆		◆		◆	◆		◆	
35. Little frog		◆						◆	
36. Little frog (development)	◆		◆						
37. The band in the park	◆		◆			◆			
38. The band in the park (development)			◆						◆

TARGETING MUSIC

	INDIVIDUALS (1)	IN PAIRS (2)	IN GROUPS (G)	AS A CLASS (C)		2				
	1	2	G	C	b	a	b	c	d	e
Playing with sounds and rhythm				◆	◆	◆	◆			
1. My baby's crying	◆			◆	◆	◆	◆	◆		
2. Move your fingers, move your thumbs		◆		◆			◆	◆		
3. Sail my ship	◆		◆	◆		◆	◆			
4. In the morning				◆			◆		◆	
5. Peter hammers with one hammer	◆		◆	◆			◆	◆		
6. My animals	◆			◆				◆		◆
7. Roll the ball	◆						◆	◆	◆	
8. The swing	◆			◆	◆	◆	◆	◆	◆	
9. Up and down the staircase	◆				◆	◆				
10. It's my birthday	◆			◆			◆			
11. I hear thunder	◆			◆			◆	◆		
12. My name is Luke		◆		◆			◆		◆	
13. Sleep, baby sleep	◆			◆	◆	◆	◆			
14. Hush-a-bye my little babe				◆			◆			
15. Our lollipop lady	◆			◆			◆			◆
16. The body song				◆			◆			◆
17. Play the drum like this	◆			◆			◆			◆
18. Worm	◆		◆	◆	◆	◆	◆		◆	
19. Put your hands together says Mrs Potato	◆			◆						◆
20. Join hands in a ring	◆			◆			◆	◆		
21. Colours	◆			◆			◆			◆
22. Train coming							◆		◆	◆
23. The elephant on a spider's web			◆	◆			◆		◆	
24. Splish, splash, splosh				◆						◆
25. Wind and sun	◆			◆						◆

TARGETING MUSIC

A year-by-year series for teachers in primary schools

A major new series of books initiated by Dorothy Taylor, addressing the needs of the music curriculum in primary education. Assembled for use by teachers without specialist training but wishing to use their own abilities – however modest, as singers or players – to deliver a musically rich diet to classes in their charge.

Key Stage 1 User's Guide

Inside this booklet you will find charts to help you plot usage of the *Targeting Music* books and CD against coverage of the National Curriculum (England)

Reception Year (age 4-5) ED 12445
Dorothy Taylor

This is the first book in the series. With plentiful guidance for the teacher, it lays a foundation of musical experience through integrated activities and a repertoire of songs and singing games. It aims throughout to encourage a feeling for music and to cultivate a sensitive listening ear.

Year 1 (age 5-6) ED 12449
Dorothy Taylor

Building on the book for Reception Year, here are 38 model lessons approaching music through the fundamental musical experiences: exploring and creating, listening and performing. The encouragement of active listening is central.

Year 2 (age 6-7) ED 12456
Dorothy Taylor and Jo Brockis

In this the third book of the series, the programme for Year 2 develops more sustained and challenging learning experiences. Attuned to the National Curriculum, content is organised through the musical elements: sound, silence, dynamics, rhythm, pitch, timbre, texture and structure.

A CD - **ED 12483** is available to supplement the first three *Targeting Music* books (covering the infant years). It contains all of the original songs, and also short extracts covering most of the listening suggestions in the text.

Dorothy Taylor is one of our foremost educators. She has extensive teaching experience in primary schools, and compiled the *Learning with Traditional Rhymes* series for Ladybird Books. She has taught at the University of London Institute of Education, and continues to lecture and write extensively. Latterly she has worked as a music adviser and inspector for Essex Local Education Authority.

Jo Brockis is Adviser for Music with the Essex Development and Advisory Service. She has taught in both primary and secondary schools, and has considerable experience in music advisory work for primary schools.

SCHOTT

48 Great Marlborough Street, London W1V 2BN
Tel: (0171) 437 1246 Fax: (0171) 437 0263

Marketing/Sales Department: Brunswick Road, Ashford, Kent TN23 1DX
Tel: (01233) 628987 Fax: (01233) 610232